THE

ATTITUDES

Keys to Prosperity and Success

John S. Rollins

For information:
MOTIV8U of North Central Florida
4600 NW 143rd Street
Gainesville, FL 32606

www.youareimportant.net

www.xulonpress.com

Ms. Clark,

Pursue your Purpose with Passion. Make a difference on Purpose.

[signature]

'18

For:

All of the people who have ever lived in Copeland.

It does take a village to raise a child –
you have done your part.

Acknowledgement

—◦◦◦—

It is an amazing feeling when someone knows that throughout his or her life, there has been a gentle force providing wind for their sails. That is how I feel about my life. There have been so many people who have been divinely appointed for my life and stationed along the path God has called me to. If I were to attempt to list them all, there is no way that I could do so. But there are several people who have done more than just provided wind. They have helped me to build the boat, hoist the sails, and steer the ship.

Mom and Dad, thank you for your prayers and your guidance and for believing in all of your children. 'Rev', I hope that as you see this now, you realize that you did not make a mistake by continually supporting me. Pastor Buck and Auntie 'Nay', thanks for your wisdom during the storms of my sailing. CJ, you are a great big brother and you make a difference. Betty, Mary, and Beverly, your resiliency inspires me. Pastor and Prophetess, thank you for providing an example on earth. To my Inner Circle – you know who you are and you know how much I value all that you are and all that you do. Laverne and MarQuelle, thank you for taking time out of your busy schedule to "check it out" and make it better.

Nikia, and Jay-R, I can only imagine what you all have put up with while I followed the call. I pray that you will never forget that I depend on you to keep me grounded. Madeleine, when God decided to give me the privilege of having you for a daughter, He blessed my life beyond my greatest imagination. MoJo, I am so proud of you. This is just the beginning of what God has in store for you. Don't ever stop.

Faye, you are my "good thing" – a physical manifestation of the joy that God has given to me. I hope that I give you as much of a reason to reach for the heavens as you have given me.

Father, most of all I thank You for Your divine plan. I am grateful that You saw that You could go to Copeland and find another vessel who would make himself available through which you could reveal Yourself.

THE

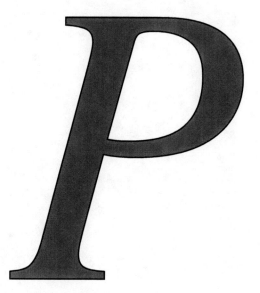

ATTITUDES

Keys to Prosperity and Success

Foreword

Johns S. Rollins is a leader of great distinction who has the potential to impact his generation in tremendous ways. I believe that with the gifting and many talents John possesses, there are no limits to the degree that he is able to touch lives. John has made an impact on my life from the first day I met him and he continues to amaze me. When I observe him, I see a man who has a love for his family, a respect for authority, and a desire to help those in need. John is a peacemaker and he is someone who says, "…you can use me, just ask."

The word that comes to mind when I think of John is practical. Practical comes from the word 'practice', which you will discover is one of the P Attitudes mentioned in this book. A practical person obtains this trait through practice or action. However, I believe this meaning fits John best; to be used or useful. It is someone who is designed for use. Another meaning of practical that describes Mr. Rollins is a concern with the application of knowledge to a useful end, rather than speculation. John makes himself available to be useful in any capacity that is needed. John is a skillful instructor in training on how to become a leader. His life is the best teacher because he practices what he teaches. His disposition demonstrates the heart of a team player and he is leading by example for others to follow. He is the kind of team member that everyone desires to have in their corner.

I highly recommend the reading and application of this book. You will experience the life changing concepts that will stay with you for a lifetime. In the years ahead, you will be able to reflect back on the principles in this book and once again be energized to view life with a healthier attitude.

This book is only the beginning of what pleasures the world will experience as they read through each page and discover that the *"P Attitudes - Keys to Prosperity and Success"* provide readers with skills to improve their inter-personal relationships. I commend John for the wealth of knowledge he has shared to help all of us become better human beings.

Dr. Horace L. Mingo
Senior Pastor
Jesus People Life Changing Church
Gainesville, Florida

Contents

—◦◦◦—

Introduction

—⟅∽∾⟆—

Ted W. Engstrom, in his book, *The Pursuit of Excellence*, said, "Success leaves clues." Millions of people are in search of success. Success is not some mystical, magical vapor that is only available to a select group of people. Everyday, people have successful outcomes. Better yet, even more have the opportunity to capitalize on successful conclusions. Unfortunately, many people do not know what to look for. Many overlook the clues.

I have often said the easiest way to hide something that is of value is to put it in plain view. It just makes sense. Our natural instinct tells us that if one is trying to hide something that is important, they have to lock it away in a safe or vault; in a secure and guarded location. The last place most people look for an article of great value is in something that is readily visible. They end up overlooking the most prized possession because, after all, if it was of any value, why would someone leave it out in the open?

Most people think success and prosperity require some secret combination. On the contrary, success and prosperity results from an accumulation of consistent thoughts beliefs, and intentional actions toward a worthwhile goal. This book reveals the simplicity of achieving success and prosperity; making it available for anyone who desires to have it.

Several years ago, I came up with a group of twelve carefully selected words to use for a training program designed to assist learners in acquiring certain skills for success. All of the words began with the letter "P." I originally called them the "12 Keys to Prosperity." Over time, I changed the title to "12 Keys to Career Success." One day, while reading from the Gospel of Matthew, I realized that Christ had also given some simple, yet profound insights into a life of success. Later, scholars labeled this wisdom the Beatitudes. That was my revelation. All of these words were "attitudes" that a person could apply to his or her personal life that could position the individual for success.

The *P Attitudes* are simple suggestions based on scriptural principles that outline steps to increasing one's effectiveness, personally and professionally. Many of the truths shared in this book are inspired by other authors from whom I have gleaned pearls of wisdom. Others come from my own personal experiences that have helped me throughout my growth and development process. I trust that as you read this book, you will agree that these ideas are based on truth; truth that has been tested over time and consistently stands strong. One of the beautiful things about truth is that it has the ability to stand on its own. Truth needs no crutch or support. Truth is eternal.

It is my desire that you will benefit from the wisdom imparted on these pages and be inspired to apply them to your situations to shape your attitudes. The *P Attitudes* are intended to help you live successfully and victoriously and help equip you to prosper in your relationship with God and with others. I pray that you find this book instrumental in positioning you to succeed in all that God has called you to do on earth and for heaven.

Make a difference – on purpose!

John S. Rollins

Pace

Chapter 1

—◦◦◦—

*P*ace — If only life were a sprint. How many would
change their strategy for living? We are all familiar with
someone who could be referred to as a "one-time wonder,"
a "flash in the night." Fortunately, the outcomes for many
of the major choices we have regarding this race called life
is likened more to a marathon than a 100-meter sprint. The
good news is that even if we did not have a great start, we
can still compete in the race.

Each year, millions apply for business licenses, patents,
and trademarks, thinking they have the next multi-million
dollar idea. Each year, millions have those ideas placed
back on the shelf because they were unaware of all that was
required to see their dream materialize. In Shakespeare's
The Merchant of Venice, ACT 1, SCENE 2, the speaker says,
"If to do were as easy as to know what were good to do,
chapels had been churches and poor men's cottages princes'
palaces." Let there be no mistake, it is not as easy as it seems.
But it is possible.

I have often jokingly said that my parents own a manual
that outline the steps for a successful marriage and parent-
hood. Occasionally, and only at night when the children are
asleep, they will pull it out of its safe spot to look through the
chapters to get answers for the situations they are confronted
with at the moment. What my parents have come to under-

stand is that a successful marriage, as well as the rearing of children, doesn't occur quickly. It requires taking one day at a time. When you act too hastily over an action

> *When you act too hastily over an action of a spouse or a child, you may damage future growth for each.*

of a spouse or a child, you may damage future growth for them.

How many times have we acted abruptly, only to regret it later? How many times have we made rash decisions without gathering all of the facts? Decisions make a difference. As a matter of fact, I will go as far as to say decisions make the difference. I have come to understand that there are some actions, words, and decisions that "oops" or "I'm sorry" will not fix. As much as I would like to go back and undo what happened, it is impossible. I am left to deal with the consequences. If only I had waited a little longer before I acted, the outcome would have been different.

Once, Christ was at a well when a woman came to draw water. Christ asked the woman for something to drink and then engaged her in a rather personal conversation. He really got the woman's attention when He disclosed some information about her relationships. Convinced that there was something special about this man, she went back to her city and invited other members of the community to come out to see Him. The townspeople came out to hear what Christ had to say and later invited Him to spend some time with them. Christ ended up staying in the city for two days and many of the townspeople came to believe in Him.

On another occasion, Christ and His disciples were traveling to Jerusalem when they came near to a small city. The town's citizens, for some unknown reason, refused to allow them passage through the city. Two of the disciples, James and John, took exception to this rejection. "…Lord, do You want us to command fire to come down from heaven and consume them, just as Elijah did?" (Luke 9:54b NKJV). Christ rebuked them because He realized they were looking at the present condition. Christ was focused on what would happen in the future. What was the name of the city? Samaria. This was the same city that had previously welcomed Him with open arms; the city that Christ would instruct the disciples to go into and witness. Christ realized that there would be another time.

I look forward to the day when my parents will take me to their room, move the bed over, and lift that loose floorboard where the secret instruction manual has resided over all of these years, and give me my own personal copy. Until then, although I don't always know all that is required and miss it some times, I must remember that as long as I continue to say "good morning," there is still a chance to get it right. Many times, it is not the fleet of foot that win the race, but the one who knows the path and keeps the pace.

Paradigm

Chapter 2

Paradigm – I remember hearing many "so-called" marriage experts, with great intentions, espousing their wisdom to young couples – "Whatever you did to get your spouse is what you have to do to keep them." Good intentions – bad advice.

I understand their approach. The actions and qualities one seeks to display during the dating process is normally the behavior the other party has grown to love and appreciate. If one person in the relationship abruptly changes shortly after the marriage, it normally results in an unhappy spouse, marriage, and home. I am convinced, however, that if I continued to be the same person at age thirty-five that I was at age twenty-three, I will still have an unhappy spouse, marriage, and home. I have to adopt an attitude of flexibility. I have to be open to new ideas and interventions as the marriage progresses. I have to change my paradigm.

Several years ago, I heard the story of a wife; we will call her June, who was cooking a ham for the holidays. For years, the husband watched as June would cut off the end of the ham before putting the ham in the pan and into the oven. One day, he asked her about the routine. "I cut off the end of the ham because my mom always cut off the end of her ham," answered the wife. Unsatisfied with the explanation, the husband called his mother-in-law to inquire. Surprisingly, he received the same response from his mother-in-law that he got from June. By now, his curiosity was out of control. Grandmother is still alive, so they agree to call her to get a better understanding of this "less-than-rich" tradition. "Granny, we have a dilemma and I believe you can help us out. June and your daughter both cut off the end of the ham before placing it in the pan to cook. I asked them about it and they said it is a tradition that you started. So, I am curious, why did you cut off the end of your ham before cooking it?" On the other end of the line, grandma was laughing uncontrollably. "I don't know why they cut off the end of their ham before cooking it. The reason I did it was because my pan was too small."

For years, there have been practices and processes that were repeated just because "...we have always done it that way." Imagine what you would be like today if you never changed anything about your life because there was "nothing wrong with the old way." (Am I the only person who remembers polyester leisure suits?) There are many advances in technology, medicine, travel, and life today simply because someone asked, "What if?"

> *I have to be open to new ideas and interventions... I have to change the way I look at things.*

Peter was a Jew – raised in the customs of his father. All of his life, he followed the law regarding interaction with unclean things. Imagine his surprise when the Lord appeared to him in a vision one afternoon while he was in prayer. Three times, a sheet was lowered from heaven with all kinds of food and a voice instructed him, "'Rise Peter, kill and eat." "Not so, Lord! For I have never eaten anything common or unclean." And a voice spoke to him again the second time, "What God has cleansed you must not call common.'" (Acts 10:13b-15 NKJV)

Through this vision, God prepared Peter to change his outlook on his view towards certain people. Peter was prompted to expect something new, something different, something never before dreamed of. From the time of Moses, it was unthinkable for salvation to be available to anyone other than a Jew. However, God, in His infinite wisdom, now declares that the time has come to change how we think about things. The way it used to be has been revised. Someone might say, "If it is not broken, then there is no need to fix it." But if there is a better way, one that is established by God, we would be unwise to not rethink our approach.

Passion

Chapter 3

*P*assion – Even the smallest of effort in pursuit of a worth-while goal is beneficial. Even the smallest excuse for failing to pursue a worthwhile goal is detrimental. For many, there is something you love doing so much that you would do it for free if you had to. The reality is that when you love doing something, you give it your best. When you give something your best, people will reward you for it. Many times the reward is financial, other times, the reward is promotion. But be assured – passion does produce a reward.

How can one tell when someone is passionate about a thing? Is it demonstrated by what a person says? Or is it only apparent by what a person does? One thing is for sure – when someone is passionate about something, there is little doubt about it by onlookers.

One of the best examples of passion I can think of comes from a young man who attends my church. When I say 'young man', I literally mean a young man; he just recently turned six years old. His passion is playing the drums. Over the last three years, I have watched as he continued to perfect his skill. He travels with a pair of drumsticks. He beats on the floor. He beats on the pews. A couple of times, I think I even saw him beat on a few people. Anywhere he thought he could get a sound, he would beat on it with his drumsticks. Other drummers have come and gone but he remains a constant.

The day I realized this young man was truly passionate about beating the drums was one morning when he left his sticks at home. Just like clockwork, he glanced over his shoulders to see if his mom was looking and off he went to the drum set. The older drummers have a shelf on which they store extra sticks. He was too short to reach it, but he refused to allow his height to become a limitation to him fulfilling his desire. I watched him climb on the drummer's stool, tiptoe and reach as high as he could, with the agility and balance of a high wire tightrope walker, fingers stretched to the limit, to grab the pouch where the additional sticks were stored. He got down, placed the headset over his ears and struck up a beat.

I remembered thinking to myself, "I wish more people were as passionate about the things that are required of them as this young man was about beating the drums." More people should adopt the posi-

One thing is for sure – when someone is passionate about a thing, there is little doubt about it by onlookers.

tion of not being denied – I have to reach my goal. There is something inside of me that I must accomplish and I will overcome any and all odds. That is the attitude of a passionate person.

Daniel was passionate about his relationship with his God. Daniel chose the ways of the Living God repeatedly and each time, his God proved that Daniel made the right choice. In fact, Daniel's passion for Jehovah was so evident that the only area where Daniel's enemies could find "fault" with Daniel was concerning the law of his God. Daniel did not do a lot of talking about how determined he was to serve God. He, as some of the young people from my church used to say, was "bout it." Daniel's passion for God caused him some heartache with some of the area's locals, but Daniel's passion was unquestionable; and Daniel's God always came through.

Patience

Chapter 4

———∽∾∿∽———

*P*atience – If anyone has ever planted a crop, you understand that you do not plant the seed and see the harvest in the same day. It takes time. Remember, if you want to see the rose bloom, you cannot keep pulling the plant out of the ground to look at the root. You have to be patient and allow the natural cycle to run its course.

I have often wondered, what is it that makes a farmer go out to the fields, spend days, maybe weeks, preparing the soil, sowing thousands of tiny seeds – some of which are so small, she can fit hundreds of them in her hand – in anticipation of a harvest to be reaped months later. Is it faith? Is it patience? Or, is it a belief in a principle God established, long, long ago – "While the earth remains, Seedtime and harvest, cold and heat, winter and summer, and

> *Remember, if you want to see the rose bloom, you cannot keep pulling the plant out of the ground to look at the root.*

day and night shall not cease" (Genesis 8:26 NKJV). In a time when so many people are seeking get-rich-quick schemes, or the next great invention, many others understand that there still is a proven formula. When you do the things you are supposed to do, when you are supposed to do them, you can expect a favorable outcome.

One of the things I used to love to see when I watched farmers was the slow, unhurried attitude with which they approached life. Not many things seemed to bother them. It seemed that everything always worked out – in time. I can vividly remember seeing the farmer stopping and releasing, what seemed at the time, a deeply satisfying sigh, taking the hat from her head, pulling a handkerchief, or in some cases a wash cloth, out of her back pocket and wiping the sweat from her forehead. Somehow, her actions communicated, "I have done everything I can do up to this point. Now, I have to just wait and see what happens." In the Scriptures, the Apostle James understood the value of patience. "But let patience have its perfect work, that you may be perfect and complete, lacking nothing" (James 1:4 NKJV).

Joshua was the leader of the Israelites. He was confronted with a wall that seemed impenetrable. When he sought God for instructions on an approach to take to secure a victory in battle, he received a strategy, which to the commander of the army, probably seemed a little foreign. He was told to gather the choir, put them in front of the army, march up to the wall, have a silent choir rehearsal, take a lap around the exterior of the wall, and go home. Repeat this process for six consecutive days and do not change a thing. On the seventh day, however, you are to follow the same process, but this time bring the musicians, light some candles, and when you walk around the wall, have everyone make as much noise as they can. On the seventh day, the walls of Jericho crumbled to the ground.

If at any time during that week of rehearsal and preparation, Joshua had become impatient with the process, the outcome would not have been pleasant. One could easily understand if Joshua were to question the approach. Obviously, this was not logical. Of course, how logical is it to think that someone can take a bag of seeds, place them in the ground, leave them there for several weeks and then come back later to find enough food in the field to feed a community?

There is a certain confidence one walks in when she knows that she is following a successful format. "I have properly prepared the soil where the seeds are to be sown, removing anything that could possibly be a distraction or a deterrent from a successful harvest. I have selected the right seed for the season; I have watered the seeds and provided them with enough light to grow. Eventually, I am going to have a crop. I cannot always control whether the seed will produce a thirty, sixty, or one-hundred fold return, but I can be guaranteed of one thing, I will have a harvest from my seeds. All I have to do is be patient and give it enough time."

Peaceful

Chapter 5

Peaceful – For me, a peaceful environment is of greater worth than a year's salary. Of course, considering my salary, there are many things that may be more valuable. My point is this – there are some things that cannot be purchased. Peace of mind is one of those things.

One of the treasures I have come to appreciate more, as the time between my birthdays seem to grow shorter, is the community where I was raised. I am sure not many people have heard of Copeland Settlement in Gainesville Florida. To this day, we still do not have a traffic light in Copeland. Even now I smile just thinking of it. In that little community, most of our neighbors were the kind of people who would make a great television show.

On one side for neighbors, we had the Watts. If I were to create my own dictionary, I would place a picture of them next to the word *neighbor*. "Daddy Watts", as he was affectionately known to all in the community, was one of the kindest, most gentle men I have ever known. I remember hearing him at a marriage seminar sharing with the group that he and his wife had been married for many, many years and he had never raised his hand or his voice to her. While that should have been the norm for the day, unfortunately, I know that was not the case. His wife, known to the community members as "Momma Watts", was a quiet, godly woman. I don't ever remember hearing her yell at any of the neighborhood kids about a ball bouncing in her garden or shrubbery – not once.

For a neighbor on the other side was the community's grocery store, owned by Mrs. Glasper. Although Mrs. Glasper did not live in the community, she was there almost every day. Mrs. Glasper was a retired school teacher who was a highly educated woman and required the same of my siblings and me. She was a woman of discipline, but I always knew that I could count on her to be fair. Mrs. Glasper rewarded me for my grades and gave me one of my first jobs. Because of the peaceful environment I experienced as a child, I am a better neighbor, a more respected employee, and a preserver of peace for my family.

Naomi and Ruth were distressed. While in a foreign land, during a famine, Naomi lost her husband and sons. After the famine was over, Naomi was able to return to her homeland and her daughter-in-law, Ruth accompanied her. However, there was no heir in Naomi's lineage to sustain the family's name. Ruth was introduced to Boaz, who had heard of Ruth's devoted lifestyle to her mother-in-law. When the situation appeared to be at its worse, Boaz comforted Ruth and assured her that everything would work out; he would seek out a peaceful resolution. "And now my daughter, do not fear. I will do for you all that you request, for all the people of my town know that you are a virtuous woman" (Ruth 3:11 NKJV). Ruth and Naomi were put at peace because of Boaz's determination to redeem the right of the inheritance.

Christ said that he would give his disciples a brand of peace that was different from any kind of peace they had ever experienced.

> *There are some things that cannot be purchased. Peace of mind is one of those things.*

He promised that He would not take peace away from the

world, that He would leave it behind. As a result of His promise, we have no need to be fearful or afraid. We can be at peace in this present world and live with an expectation of eternal peace.

Peculiar

Chapter 6

—◈—

Peculiar – "You are unlike anyone I have ever seen." If someone makes that comment to you, do you wonder if it is a compliment? When did that statement become an insult? Somewhere along the way, it became "uncool" to be different. I am not sure if it was the result of peer pressure from other students at school, competition between the corporations to succeed in the marketplace, or just because it is easier to conform than it is to resist the urge to bow down.

I believe each individual possesses something that makes him or her special – something unique. There are attributes that each of us possess that make us important. Part of the challenge is identifying and celebrating those specific characteristics or traits that separate us from the crowd. Too often, we depend on, require, or expect someone else to validate us by acknowledging our worth. While it feels good to be recognized by others for what we are or what we possess, I have found that many times we put an unfair amount of pressure on other people or on ourselves when we wait for them to assess our value.

There is someone, however, who has already communicated to us just how important we are and is constantly sharing with us how He views us. He constantly reminds us that it was His original intention to make us with individual

> *We are a matchless creation especially formed by a Matchless Creator.*

traits that help form our identity. He also gave us instructions for those areas where we are to be similar and He provided the technique for meeting His requirements. It is not now, nor was it ever His intention, that we become just another faceless, nameless, identity-less person in the crowd.

One day, God hosted a meeting. When the invited guests arrived, there was also an unexpected guest who decided to attend – Satan. In the ensuing conversation, the topic came up about the inhabitants of the earth. It is God's statement to Satan that convinces me that God distinguishes us as individuals. He asked Satan, "Have you considered My servant Job, that there is none like him on the earth, a blameless and upright man, one who fears God and shuns evil?" (Job 1:8 NKJV)

God clearly revealed, during this conversation with the Adversary, that there is something that each of us possesses – something unique that God knows He has placed within us. There is something that makes us unlike any other person who occupies this earth. In these situations, this uniqueness is recognized and celebrated by God and causes God to select us for special assignments where He can display us as victorious, overcoming vessels of honor for Him. Of course, I can imagine someone thinking, "If I have to deal with what Job had to deal with, I am not sure I want to be picked out because of the things that make me different." My statement to you – if God thinks enough of you to select you as His contender to represent Him in a battle against the enemy, I guarantee that God believes in you.

One morning, my daughter and I were discussing her individuality. I took a handful of coins and asked her to select one that was to represent her. I then took that coin and mixed it in with several other coins that looked like the coin that represented her and asked her to find herself among the other coins. She was unable to do so. "Why not," I asked. "Because they all look the same," she said. From that exchange, I was able to get her to understand that in God's eyes, we were never intended to be lost in the crowd. We are a matchless creation especially formed by a Matchless Creator. She was, as are you, created to be a special, unique creation – a peculiar person, unlike any other.

People

Chapter 7

—◦◦◦—

People – I have often heard it said that 85% of the success of an organization is a result of the quality of the relationships between the people. Technical skills or competency, reportedly, has only a 15% impact on the organization's success. If those statistics are true, then many companies have misdirected their efforts. Instead of focusing attention on developing a catchy advertising or marketing campaign, maybe time and money would be better spent on selecting the right people to be part of the team. After all, how many times has it been said, "People are our greatest asset."

I have come to understand that *people* are not an organization's greatest asset – unless they are the *right people*. It is true, people come a dime a dozen. But the right person, like an eagle, is a rare find. And attracting and keeping the right person or people should be the focus of every organization desiring to go to the next level.

A gentleman, whom I have had the privilege of working with quite closely over the last 30 years, reminded me of the importance of having the right people on the team. Unfortunately, the price he paid for the lesson was his health and his job. He was the district manager of twenty-eight offices and franchises. He had over four hundred employees reporting to him, serving over thirty-four thousand clients. For five years, his district led the state in productivity, amassing nearly four million dollars per year in sales. Each year his team realized double digit increases. He had a highly functional team composed of people who knew his vision, bought into it and delivered amazing results.

> *Attracting and keeping the right person or people should be the focus of every organization desiring to go to the next level.*

After several years, the team started to dismantle. One person retired. Another person was promoted. Another member left to follow a spouse who was transferred. What my friend discovered was that unless you have the right people in the positions that matter most, the success you experienced cannot be maintained. My friend worked harder and put in longer hours, but it was just a matter of time. Hard work could not make up the difference over the long haul. Because the team was not composed of the right people, his health suffered and he was relieved of that responsibility.

Gideon was called to deliver the Israelites from the oppression of the Midianites. After he was finally convinced that God was going to use him, he gathered a group of soldiers to escort him into battle. Thirty-two thousand men physically walked away from the camp. It is important to understand that every person who dons your team's colors is not committed to the call at hand. Of those men who followed Gideon, twenty-two thousand left their minds and hearts back in the camp. Of the remaining ten thousand, 9,700 of them were not fully focused on the task at hand. Through a divine selection process, God eliminated all of the people who were unnecessary to secure the victory. God was able to victoriously liberate the Israelites with three hundred people who wanted to be there. These men were not afraid to tackle a monumental challenge and they were fully focused on one thing – getting back home to their families.

Once a team has the right people, the next step is to train and develop them. Whether we acknowledge it or not, we all need people and people need us. According to Zig Ziglar, "You can get anything you want out of life if you help enough other people get what they want out of life." There may be security in numbers; however, success is not necessarily achieved unless you have the right people factored into the equation.

Perfection

Chapter 8

———❧❧❧———

Perfection – The old saying, "Practice makes perfect," is not completely true. But of even greater importance is the concept of not striving for perfection but striving for progress. Don't allow anyone to pressure you into thinking that everything has to be perfect, and do not put that unnecessary pressure on yourself. Today, you want to be farther along toward your goals than you were yesterday. In order to accomplish that, however, you must have goals.

For decades, plastic surgery has been viewed as the method of choice in the pursuit of the perfect size, the perfect face, the perfect body, the perfect complexion. It is unfortunate that so many people feel the need to be different than who they were created to be in order to be accepted by others. I have heard of stories of patients dying on the operating table because they wanted a different body and were willing to risk everything in pursuit of the perfect look. Surely I am not suggesting there aren't other factors involved in making these decisions. But I am curious to know how many times pressure from other people or outside sources influence the final verdict.

As a sports fan, I often listen to sports radio talk shows. Although I find many of the shows informative, and at times entertaining, on many occasions I have turned the radio off or switched to a different station because of the judgmental comments of the host as he or she criticized another person's efforts, intentions, or decisions. It was so easy for the show's host to pass judgment on the athletes, who in the heat of the competition, failed to perform up to their expectations. The athlete's mistakes were critiqued mercilessly. I understand the business. In order to keep the show on the air, there has to be listeners. The audience longs for the opportunity to hear and share comments that reveal different, and yes, controversial opinions. The show becomes entertaining to the audience when the host pits two opposing opinions against each other and then gets the listeners to chime in, supporting one of the two perspectives.

Christ was called to issue a ruling between a woman who had been caught with a man who was not her husband by some of the religious leaders of the day. According

> *In life we do not have the luxury of an instant replay.*

to the law, the woman was to be condemned and put to death by stoning. The "talk-show" hosts had all of the facts they needed and were waiting for the go ahead to take the woman to the rock quarry. In their minds, this woman was beyond correction – she would never meet up to the established standards. Christ provided an effective method for conflict resolution – let the perfect people lead the charge for stoning the guilty person. He did not deny the lady was wrong in what she did. He did not dispute that she may have deserved the punishment. Instead, He helped her accusers understand that perfection is a state that not many of us will attain in our lifetime while here on earth. When the woman's accusers "got the message" they left her alone with Christ. His message to her was a simple one. "You are not perfect, but do not accept that as a crutch. Tomorrow and in the future, you are to be farther along than where you are today."

In the day of slow motion and instant replay, it is easy to second guess someone's action or decision. If the referee misses the first call, he can call timeout, call up to the booth, and watch the play in slow motion, repeatedly, from different angles, get input from several other people, and finally, after several minutes of review, hopefully get the call right. However, regardless of the decision, half of the people will like the call – half of the people will want to take him out to the woodshed for a shellacking.

In life, we do not have the luxury of instant replay. Sometimes we get the call right, sometimes we miss it. When we get it right, we keep playing until the next decision point. When we miss it, we stop, make the necessary corrections, pray the damage was minor, and get back on the right track and take every measure to avoid making that mistake again. That is progress, not perfection.

Persistence

Chapter 9

—⟨∿∿⟩—

Persistence – Calvin Coolidge said, "Nothing in the world can take the place of persistence. Talent will not; nothing is more common than unsuccessful men with talent. Genius will not; unrewarded genius is almost a proverb. Education will not; the world is full of educated derelicts. Persistence and determination alone are omnipotent." The *Encarta® World English Dictionary, North American Edition* defines persistence as the, "quality of persisting: the quality of continuing steadily despite problems or difficulties."

One of my favorite movies is *The Shawshank Redemption*. There are several subplots in the movie, but the theme that I am drawn to more than

> *When one is committed to a cause, there is no room for distraction or deterrents.*

any other is Tim Robbins' unwillingness to accept his status as an imprisoned man. As a result of his determination, he devises a plan, secures the necessary resources, aligns himself with the people who can assist him, and begins the process. For him the cause is a worthy one. Therefore, time is irrelevant. With a dogged resolve he continues toward the goal – one spoon of dirt; one pocketful of rocks. Every day, the hole gets larger and the tunnel gets longer. Steadily, in between counts, in between bed checks, he is getting closer to the destination, until the night that he reclaims his freedom.

What is it that keeps a person going, despite the odds that seem stacked against them? When there are so many voices yelling for them to stop, what keeps them going full speed ahead? Why is it that a "No" will stop some, but not others? When one is committed to a cause, there is no room for distraction or deterrents.

That was the case for one woman born in the city of Greece. This Syro-Phoenician woman, whose young daughter had an unclean spirit, came to Christ asking Him to cast the demon out of her daughter. Initially, it seemed that Christ ignored her, but she was not to be denied. She made a "pest" of herself, insisting not only to be heard, but to receive the one thing for which she came – deliverance for her daughter.

Once she was able to get Christ to respond to her, He did not give her the answer she wanted to hear. "But Jesus said to her, 'Let the children be filled first; for it is not good to take the children's bread and throw it to the little dogs'" (Mark 7:27 NKJV). It would have been completely under-standable for her to walk away rejected – feeling sorry for herself and for her daughter. A negative response from the one person on the entire earth who could make a difference in the life of her daughter could have been devastating, but she persisted. Not being a Calvin Coolidge enthusiast, I can neither confirm nor deny that he considered this story when he said "…Persistence and determination alone are omnipotent." The mother in this story is the embodiment of those traits mentioned in Coolidge's quote. As a result, she realized the fulfillment of her desire; her daughter was delivered.

Throughout our lives, we hear so many negative statements – "You had better not do that," "Stop it!" "You can't go there," "You can't do that," "I don't believe you will make it," and the list goes on and on. Sometimes, we have to turn a deaf ear to all of the naysayer's and press on. Such was the case for the little engine, climbing the mountain with a load bigger than it had ever carried before. His destiny awaited him on the other side. Had he not believed he could make it, had he not pressed on, had he not persisted, he never would have made it.

Perspective

Chapter 10

—❦—

Perspective – I have many questions – about many things, as I am sure each of us does. Where am I to go to find the answers to the questions that often paralyze me? How am I to know if I am on the right track regarding the decisions of life? I have found that for almost any question regarding the challenges life offers, there are several sources and many different perspectives for which one can find possible solutions. Some of my answers I found around me. Other answers, I found within me. Most of my answers were found above me.

In counseling sessions, I have often been credited with changing the way a person thinks or acts. I am often uncomfortable with that statement because my intention is very seldom, if ever, to change someone. As a goal, I have the desire to take the individual from one side of the problem, issue, opportunity, or challenge, and allow them to view it from a different angle – another perspective. How many times have we heard, "Well, it all depends on how you look at it?" It really does matter on an individual's perspective.

In my late teens or early twenties (it has been some time since both of those milestones in my life) I distinctly remember trying to come up with a single word that described me. If someone were to ask me to use one word to help them understand me, what would it be? Of all of the possibilities –

assertive, distinguished, gregarious, flamboyant, compassionate, the word I settled on was "balanced." I realized, even at that point in my life, that there were going to be some moments when things would go very well for me, and other occasions when I would not like the outcome. It was at that point that I decided that I could control, or choose, how I viewed a situation or a set of circumstances. Since arriving at that decision, I have had some truly wonderful experiences to impact my life – things that were deserving of celebration and recognition. I

> *Some of my answers I find around me. Other answers I find within me. Most of my answers were found above me.*

was always able to remember that these were good days and I was to enjoy them, but I was to not get too excited. I have also had moments that were hugely disappointing – the kind that caused me to question the will to continue to go on. I remembered that these were sad days, and to not get too down. As long as I did not stop in the "storm," I would get through it.

Job was a man who had a good life, according to the standards for his time. His family was wealthy and they had a strong relationship. One day, Job's circumstances took an unexpected turn for the worse. He lost his family members and the family's fortune all in the same day. Given those conditions, one could easily understand if Job entered into a manic depressive state. Job's response, however, was to realize that he alone controlled how he viewed the situation. That was not the end of it for Job. Not long after, his health was attacked. His wife offered one perspective that differed from Job's vantage point. Job chose to ignore her input. Later, some close business associates came for a visit to shed some light on what they saw. They aimed to get Job to see things from their point of view. Once again, Job's decision was to see his condition from a different perspective.

Job remained steadfast in how he chose to assess his state of affairs. Eventually, Job's health, fortune, and family was restored, all because he chose to keep a proper perspective on the events that affected his life. Life, like an assorted bag of jelly beans, comes in many colors and flavors. Just as each of us gets to choose our favorite flavors, we also get to choose our perspective on life.

Plan

Chapter 11

*P*lan – I have heard it said so many times before – "People do not plan to fail. People fail to plan." Very few people actually set out to fail. So what is it that makes the difference between a successful effort and one that is unsuccessful? Sometimes, it's circumstances – changes in the economy, politics, the market, or some other factor. Other times, it may be leadership – people do make a difference. However, more often than not, the thin line that defines successful and unsuccessful ventures is the plan. Victorious individuals and teams plan the work and work the plan.

While fate seems to control the destiny of so many people, those people with a plan seem to control their own fate. Whether it is a business plan for a Fortune 500 company, a game plan for the Super Bowl, or a work plan for a new employee, the outcome is best realized when the plan has been carefully thought out. A great plan, one made with the right intentions and for the right reason, eventually triumphs over an evil plan.

Haman, after feeling spurned by Mordecai's refusal to bow down to him, approached the King of Shushan with an evil plot to extinguish the Jews. Once Haman's scheme was publicized, Mordecai's initial reaction was to panic. Sensing the gravity of the situation, Mordecai understood that panicking would be of little value to him or his relatives. Mordecai realized he needed a plan.

Employing every resource available to him and capitalizing on all the influence he had been able to garner among the people, Mordecai sent a message to Esther, the queen, informing her of Haman's

> *More often than not, the thin line that defines successful and unsuccessful ventures is the plan.*

grudge and imploring her to seek the king's assistance in squashing this genocidal plot. Although Esther seemed reluctant to participate at first, Mordecai reminded her that something would be done to save the nation of the Jews. He assured the queen that because of her heritage, her fate would be the same as his if she did not work the plan. That's where a good plan became a great one. Esther responded with an addendum to the plan. She told Mordecai that she, along with all of her attendants, were going on a fast. She asked that all of the Jews in the region also fast. After three days, she would approach the king. When the opportunity came, Esther exposed Haman's dastardly plot, Haman was executed, and the nation of the Jews was spared.

It takes a lot of time and effort to work through all of the details to come up with a good plan. It takes a lot more time and effort to redo the work that was done poorly as a result of someone refusing to properly plan the job. As a child, I remember hearing a wise man say, "Why is there never enough time to do the job right, but there is always time to do the job over again?" Spend twice as much time measuring so you do not have to spend as much time sawing. That is the key to a great plan.

Polite

Chapter 12

Polite – If you were to ever approach my children and ask them about Daddy's rules for respect, this is what you will hear. "I am to always make sure that I respect two people – myself and the other person." I have come to understand that if you treat people politely and show them respect, you will receive extended favor and forgiveness from them – even when you don't deserve it.

Although I am sure there are exceptions, it is difficult for me to think of any situation where a person did not deserve to be treated politely and with respect. I also understand that the decision of how I choose to treat people rests completely with me. I can choose my response to the circumstances. Believe me, I know there are some people who present challenges to this rule, but regardless of how complicated the situation may be, I still assert that the final decision rests with each individual.

Life is complicated. Situations are challenging. Unfortunately, people don't always behave appropriately. Things happen – sometimes, traumatic things. Amazingly, there are

> *Those persons acknowledge that they cannot always control what life does to them, but they alone can choose how they respond.*

some people who seem to take the worst that life has to offer and use it as fuel to get them through the obstacle and propel them forward. They take what looks like the most unfortunate situation and the most terrible actions that come out of people, and appear unfazed in their response to those circumstances – in how they choose to view others. I am convinced this is not a coincidence but rather a conscious choice. It is as if those persons acknowledge that they cannot always control what life does to them, but they alone can choose how they respond.

Isaac was instructed by his Lord to remain in an unfruitful land. Because of God's promise, however, Isaac was able to prosper in the land. Although there was a famine in the land, Isaac became very wealthy. Because of Isaac's success, several people became envious. The king of the land where Isaac dwelt became afraid and demanded that Isaac leave the country. Isaac did not speak ill of the king. When Isaac settled in another part of the country he dug wells to support his family and flock. His enemies clogged his wells. He dug other wells, and the enemies clogged those as well. It seemed that wherever Isaac went, other people wreaked havoc for him, but not once does the scripture record him ever going to war over things that he knew he could replace. I believe that because Isaac decided that he would do no evil to people, but rather be polite to his oppressors, he was continually able to receive good things from the Lord. Eventually, he found a place where he dug wells and was not under pressure from his enemies. "So he called the place Rehoboth, because he said, 'For now the Lord has made room for us, and we shall be fruitful in the land'" (Genesis 26:22b NKJV).

In the book of 2 Samuel, chapter 10, Hanun, the king of Ammon, because of an insecure disposition, treated the army of Israel with discontent. His suspicious nature kept him from receiving the kindness of King David. In fact, he had his army to insult the men in the king's army. Because of

Hanun's decision to treat David's men shamefully, David's men eventually ended up routing the entire army. What was the difference between Isaac and Hanun? The key was where they placed their security and in whom they trusted.

If my confidence and security lie within my own ability, then I am hesitant to be polite to others. My fear is that the other person may try to take advantage of my kindness. I am afraid that I am projecting a sense of weakness which will allow the other party to get an upper hand against me. As a result, the things I need and the things I desire may not be met. The other side of the equation is that when I am okay with whom I am and I rest comfortably in knowing that it is God who takes care of me and meets my needs, it is easy for me to be kind and trusting of others. I am able to be polite to others and treat them with respect.

Practice

Chapter 13

Practice – "Biscuit," the moderator called out. "Biscuit – B-I-S-C-I-U-T, Biscuit," I replied. That is incorrect. Then the moderator turned to the other finalist in the 5th grade spelling bee, Jim S. He spelled the word correctly and then he spelled, "Pioneer," a word that I also knew how to spell. It was a hard way to learn the lesson, but I assure you, I got it; I can never practice too much.

Fast forward seven years later. In my senior year of high school, one of my teachers told me that I needed to learn to type. I had all of my credits to graduate, so I agreed to be an aide for her class. Besides, there was a girl in the class that I liked. I began pecking (I used a typewriter back then). A-S-D-F, J-K-L-; I learned the home row of keys. Chapter by chapter, lesson by lesson, I improved in accuracy and speed. As I continued to improve, my teacher noticed, and asked me about participating in the Future Business Leaders of America's (F.B.L.A.) competition as a Beginner Typist. I was a two-way starter on the football team, wearing a letterman's jacket. There was no trace of

> *If there is no practice, one is guaranteed to never achieve perfection and it is highly unlikely that there will be much, if any, improvement.*

"cool" in typing, but after repeated promptings (and a few threats) I agreed. I wasn't sure of my expectations. I knew my speed was not that great, but the competition guidelines consisted of speed and accuracy. Not only did the person have to type fast, they also had to be able to spell the words correctly. It was a perfect opportunity to combine the lessons I learned from 5th grade with all that I had practiced for the contest. I placed first in the District and was allowed to represent the district in the state competition. During the state's F.B.L.A. competition, I placed second. Therefore, my practice paid off for me.

Imagine a young shepherd boy on the backside of a mountain, bored, with nothing else to do while the sheep were grazing. He picked up the two pieces of leather, with a piece of skin tied in the middle, given to him by his father, and found some rocks. He would select a target and wind that slingshot around, letting a rock fly in the direction of his intended destination. Sometimes he hit it – other times he missed, but he kept practicing. Over time, he noticed improvement in his accuracy. One day, while watching his father's sheep, David had to confront and defeat a lion. On another day, he had to defeat a bear. Now, his practice had prepared him for his biggest confrontation to date. He was across the battlefield from a fighting machine – Goliath. David approached the giant with the confidence of a kid in a candy store with his weekly allowance. He knew he had paid the price by practicing and possessed the skills he needed to get what he wanted – Goliath's head.

All of the quiet times on the backside of the mountain, target after target, rushed to his mind. He would not use a sword. He could not use a sword. That was not the way he had practiced it. Grabbing five smooth stones from a stream, he rushed toward the giant, winding the sling on the way, and letting it fly – right into the forehead of the giant. He won a victory for his nation and for his God. Practice paid off for David.

In the chapter, *Perfection*, I opened by suggesting that practice does not make perfect. It is only perfect practice that brings us closer. But here is an indisputable truth. If there is no practice, one is guaranteed to never achieve perfection and it is highly unlikely that there will be much, if any, improvement. One can also reasonably conclude that when they practice, considering that the technique is sound, they have a good coach and commits to the process, they will be better at the end of the day than they were at the beginning.

Prayer

Chapter 14

—∿∿—

*P*rayer – "Lord, teach us how to pray, as John taught his disciples to pray," one of the disciples requested. (Luke 11:1 KJV) It was as if the disciples finally came to realize that there must be something to gain from praying; something that could be personally beneficial. The disciples understood that Jesus performed signs and miracles that were unlike anyone they had ever seen or heard about. The disciples looked for something that could explain the difference between what Christ could do and what they actually did. They observed him closely for some time. It was not His diet; they ate with Him. It was not His sleeping and resting schedule; they were with Him day and night. The only thing they could discern that explained the difference between what He did and what they did was the amount of time He spent in prayer and the manner in which He prayed. They wanted to know how to do it so they could get the same results Christ did.

One of the things my parents taught my siblings and me early in life was to memorize the Lord's Prayer. I am not sure if they taught it to us because they wanted us to know how to pray or because they just wanted us to pray. For years, I recited that prayer, not knowing that I could establish a relationship with God as my Father. Instead of viewing Him as some distant being, who only resided in heaven, He wanted me to know Him as a constant companion who was genuinely and intimately interested in all of the affairs of my life.

Over time, as my understanding of who God was grew and I recognized how strongly He wanted to be in continuous communication with me, my method of prayer changed. Not only did my method change but I also came to understand that there were no topics concerning my life that were off limits. I understood that God already knew everything that could possibly be known about my life – things that I was conscious of and things that were deeply hidden in my inner most being. I had no reason to be ashamed or uncomfortable coming to Him in prayer asking Him for help to make me become more like Him.

There have been many occasions, and I suspect there will be many more in the future, when it occurred to me that I needed to pray. I have been awakened in the middle of the night, or driving down the road, sometimes while sitting at my desk, other times I may have been out on the lake fishing. Sometimes, the prayer was about me – "God, there is something going on in me that I do not understand. I know that you made me and whatever this thing is about me that is causing me so much confusion, please reveal it to me." Other times, I would pray about or for other people who may have been experiencing sickness or challenges. I have prayed for things and for situations. There was no area where I placed a limit on what I would ask of God. On many occasions, I saw an immediate response to my prayer. In other situations, there was no external response at all, just a calming effect that took place within me.

On one occasion, King Herod decided to bring oppression to the Church by imprisoning James and Peter. He killed James and when he saw that the Jews were pleased, he planned to kill Peter also. What Herod did not know, however, was that the church was praying for Peter's safety. During the night, while Peter calmly slept between two soldiers, bound by two chains, with a prison guard on watch outside the cell, an angel of the Lord came to deliver Peter from the prison. As a result of the church's prayer, Peter's chains fell off and he was escorted through the prison without disturbing a

> *On many occasions, I saw an immediate response to my prayer. In other situations, there was no external response at all; just a calming effect that took place within me.*

single person. The heavy iron gate that guarded the city was opened without the efforts of a single individual. Peter was safely delivered to the very people who prayed for his protection.

After Christ taught them the manner in which they were to pray, a little while later He gave them the recipe for getting their prayers answered. "Therefore, I say unto you. What things soever ye desire, when ye pray, believe that ye receive them, and ye shall have them" (Mark 11:24 KJV). It is fascinating. I have been granted access to the most powerful force in all creation. I can communicate to God, through prayer.

Preparation

Chapter 15

reparation – Opportunity has the uncanny habit of
favoring those who have paid the price with years of
preparation. In all situations, those persons who become
masters of their fields are those who have paid the price
of thorough preparation. Eddie Cantor once said, "It takes
twenty years to become an overnight success."

One thing that I enjoy watching is a person who truly
values or takes great pride in the quality of his/her work. It is
a pleasure to watch someone master a particular trade
or skill. While I will never
hold any claim to fame for
my musical abilities, I have
been fortunate to work with
some really talented musicians. And there was one
distinguishing quality that
separated the group who constantly *received* calls to perform
from the group that was constantly *calling* others for the
opportunity to perform. The key was the time the artists put
into preparing their trade. Michelangelo said, "If the people
knew how hard I had to work to gain my mastery, it wouldn't
seem wonderful at all."

> *Preparation is the final
> number to the combination
> that unlocks the door to
> opportunity.*

Preparation is the final number to the combination that
unlocks the door to opportunity. It doesn't matter if you are

Bishop T.D. Jakes, practicing your sermons in the woods all alone, or if you are Tiger Woods on the driving range well into the evening, when everyone has gone home. It doesn't matter if you are Peyton Manning spending extra time in the film room after the other players have called it a day, or if you are Beyoncè going over the dance moves – again – because the timing was off just a little bit. The one thing each one of these people have in common is that they were able to capitalize on their opportunity because they paid the price of preparation.

One of the most difficult and frustrating things we will face is when we know that there is greatness within but have to remain in a state of preparedness until the opportunity comes. We often ask the question, "When will the time come?" At the age of seventeen, Joseph learned through a dream that one day his family would bow before him. Not long after, he faced abandonment by his own family and was sold into slavery. Over the next several years, Joseph had to wonder if any of it was worth it. He was falsely accused by his master's wife and imprisoned for it. Next, he was forgotten by a friend he helped succeed in his field. For thirteen years nothing seemed to come together. However, during that time, Joseph was being prepared. And when the opportunity came, Joseph left little room for doubt about who the person was that could get the job done. He positioned himself to be used mightily and God used him to save his family and the Nation of Israel. His preparation and God's favor resulted in him being appointed second in command for the entire Egyptian nation.

One of my favorite quotes comes from Zig Ziglar, who says, "I will do today what others will not do. I will do tomorrow what others cannot do." When the bullets are flying and the bombs are dropping, it is too late to prepare for the war. Prepare for war in times of peace. Opportunity will come, but normally unannounced. Be prepared.

Principle

Chapter 16

———∽∽∽———

Principle – It is unwise for one to think that violating Universal Laws will lend itself to success. There is no right way to do the wrong thing. True, long-term success, comes to those who over time, apply definite principles, not to those who are 'lucky.'

Somewhere along the way, our society quit rooting for the underdog and began celebrating the winner – even when the winner did things that violated the morals of society. It is as if we adopted the position that the only thing that mattered was the final score at the end of the game. Of course, not many people will openly admit that they want to win "at all cost," but we see it. It doesn't matter if it is a Little League World Series game where the coach allows a player to compete, even though the athlete is too old, or an Olympic competition where the competitors are seeking that extra edge by any means. The message that is being communicated is, "Well, if we put in a little additive to the fuel to give us a competitive edge, who will know?" "Why should I be the only one playing by the rules – no one else is?"

> *What we understood was that just like God's Word, North, South, East, and West were unchanging.*

There are so many conflicting messages

105

defining right and wrong. Even our decision makers in government and the church seem torn on where the line is that separates the two. For our society, I have come to understand that the farther away we get from the center line, the easier it is to blur right and wrong, good and bad, yes and no. When we make our decisions based on what the majority is doing, I am convinced that our alignment with good morals or fundamental truths is off base. There are a group of principles that will not change.

As a dispatcher with the police department, one of the early lessons I learned was how to give and receive directions. In my hometown, we used the rule of APRL for street identification and direction of travel. As a general rule Avenues, Places, Roads, and Lanes ran east to west, whereas Streets, Terraces, Boulevards, and Courts ran north and south. Whenever there was a pursuit or someone left the scene, it was of little value to know if the person ran to the left or to the right because left and right depended on which direction you were facing or how the responding unit approached the scene. In this case, left and right were relative. However, if we told a responding unit the subject was last seen headed east from NW 13th Street in the 800 block, there is no confusion about where to begin looking for the subject. What we understood was that just like God's Word, North, South, East and West were unchanging. It did not matter where we were in the city, the state, the country, or the world.

Joseph, the son of Jacob from the Scriptures, understood right and wrong. As a servant in the home of one of the nation's leaders, far away from his homeland, his definition of appropriate behavior remained unchanged. Early in his life, he was introduced to an inner compass that he would use throughout his life to guide him on how to make decisions that could be unethical. His master's wife persistently pursued him. Instead of caving in to her incessant demands, which would mean violating the fundamental principles he learned as a child and compromise the trust of his master and God, he decided that he would rather go to prison. His decision cost him his freedom, but not his integrity. Years later, he was rewarded because of his faithfulness. He was promoted and was instrumental in saving the nation of Egypt, his family, and preserving the bloodline through which Christ would later come.

David Joseph Schwartz said, "The person determined to achieve maximum success learns the principle that progress is made one step at a time. A house is built one brick at a time. Football games are won a play at a time. A department store grows bigger one customer at a time. Every big accomplishment is a series of little accomplishments." Doing the right thing, when measured against God's rule, is like North and South. North will always be in the opposite direction of South, like right will always be in the opposite direction of wrong. Consistent movement in the right direction will lead us to successful outcomes. Principles, unlike the yellow-brick road, are what we should follow to lead us back home.

Problem

Chapter 17

—◦◦◦—

*P*roblem – Problems are much like opinions; everyone has them. You don't measure a person's success or failure by how many problems they have, but rather by how they respond to those problems. It is not what happens to you – it is what happens in you. The baby that falls when learning to walk is better off than the baby that cannot learn to walk.

I have often wondered what it would be like to live in a world free of struggles and disappointments. Is it unrealistic to long for the day when the challenges cease? I think not. Thankfully, one day I will not have to wonder about that anymore. A place like that exists – it's called heaven. But until I get there, how am I supposed to approach life, knowing that every day I am confronted with situations beyond my control that don't always work out the way I desire them to?

I am aware that no one is exempt when it comes to problems. In order for me to respond appropriately, I have to decide on a method for dealing with the problems that preserves me while I go through them. Reinhold Niebuhr seemed to have a pretty good solution in his *Serenity Prayer:*

O God and Heavenly Father,
Grant to us the serenity of mind to
accept that which cannot be changed;
the courage to change that which can
be changed, and the wisdom to know
the one from the other, through Jesus
Christ our Lord, Amen.

This is the approach I have adopted. It is simply a case of "mind over matter." The mind of God overcomes the matters of the world. God's solutions overcome all of my issues. I know of times that I have come across situations where I had no idea of what the next step was. Regardless of where I searched, there seemed to be no solutions.

King Jehoshaphat was in dire distress concerning a report of several armies who were planning to attack the assembly of Judah and Jerusalem. Jehoshaphat knew that his army stood no chance in the impending battle. The only hope he had was in the God of his fathers. Like Niebuhr, Jehoshaphat consulted the Lord – seeking a solution. His

> *It is simply a case of "mind over matter." The mind of God overcomes the matters of the world.*

prayer to God went something like this – "God, we have a big problem here and we have no idea how to handle it. We have aligned ourselves with you with the expectation that you would be there for us. In fact, we decided a long time ago that, "If disaster comes upon us – sword, judgment, pestilence, or famine – we will stand before this temple and in Your presence … and cry out to You in our affliction and You will hear and save" (2 Chronicles 20:9 NKJV). God handled the problem for them. As an extra bonus, he also gave them a three-day, all-expense paid shopping spree.

We will all have problems. That is just a part of life, but we do not have to allow the problems to have us. Our confidence is in a God who is much bigger than any problem we may have. As we trust Him to deliver us, He will prove Himself faithful.

Process

Chapter 18

—◦◦◦—

*P*rocess – A famous author once said that the secret to one's success, or the secret to one's failure, is found in their daily agenda. I heard Zig Ziglar say, "You are what you are and you are where you are because of what's gone in your mind. You can change what you are and you can change where you are by changing what goes in your mind."

As a youngster I remember so clearly thinking to myself, "I can't wait until I grow up. I will be able to do whatever I want to do, whenever I want to do it." For others, it may have been going to middle school, high school, college, getting a job, getting married, having a child, or buying a house. The list goes on and on. What I have come to understand now is that when I wanted those things, I was not ready for them. While I was in middle school, there was no way that I could have handled the assignments or the relationships that were in high school. I had to develop – physically, mentally, emotionally, and academically.

Oftentimes, people think that it is easy to circumvent the process. Of course, there are many times when one can improve on the process – but there is a process. One only has to look at nature to realize that there is a step one, step two, three, four, and so on. Till the soil, plant the seed, water the ground, remove the weeds, harvest the crop, rinse and repeat. The cycle is repeated by planting more seed.

God had a process for the Israelites. He wanted them to totally and completely rely on Him. However, from their vantage point, they needed an earthly king. All of the other nations had a king and because "everyone else was doing it," the Israelites thought they needed a king too. Even though God honored their request, Israel's choice to have a king rule over them instead of the Lord disrupted the process. The first king chosen to rule over Israel ended up losing his kingdom in battle because he violated the process established by the Lord. Not only did his indiscretion impact the kingdom, his decision cost him his life, and the lives of his sons.

Righteous Noah was instructed to build an ark. God was going to destroy the earth and all of its inhabitants with a flood. Up until that time, never before had

> *There is a process...a step one, step two, three, four and so on.*

water fallen from the sky. Surely one could understand if Noah had questions regarding his assignment. Despite any misgivings, Noah gathered his supplies and began building the ark. For one hundred and nineteen years he continually obeyed the instructions given to him by the Lord, even though there was no indication that anything around him seemed different. In the following year, however, after Noah successfully completed his task and gathered the animals, God literally opened up the floodgates of heaven and poured out judgment on mankind. Because Noah precisely followed God's process, Noah, his family, and our earth as we know it today exists.

Birth always follows conception. Death will never come before Life. The end is always after the beginning. There is a natural process to all the things created by God. When we follow God's natural process, He takes responsibility for securing our successful outcomes. He promised through the Apostle Paul; "And we know that all things work together for good to those who love God, to those who are the called according to His purpose (process)" Romans 8:28 NKJV (emphasis added).

Progressive

Chapter 19

Progressive – Your ability to influence others is often at war with their ability to influence you. The longer one remains in the vicinity of the forbidden, the easier it is to justify an inappropriate action. A cold egg placed in boiling water will crack. However, when a cold egg is placed in cold water and heated to a boil over time, you can prepare for egg salad.

One of my former pastors told a story of a wealthy business owner looking to hire a driver for his family's carriage. During the interview, three prospective drivers were taken up to a high mountain with a narrow roadway next to a deadly drop off. To determine their skill level, each driver was asked how close he could drive next to the cliff without going over the edge. Boastingly, the first driver responded, "Sir, I would have no problem getting within one foot of the edge without going over." The business owner seemed impressed as he turned to the second driver. "That is nothing Sir, I can get within six inches of the edge and never lose control of the carriage." Looking to the final driver, the business owner waited to hear the response. Walking over to the edge of the cliff and peering over, the final driver looked back at the business owner and said, "Sir, have you seen the view over the edge of the hill? I would stay as far away from the edge of this cliff as possible." He was given the job.

Often, we feel the need to push our fortunes as far as possible, seeking the next thrill. If a little bit was good, a

> *If a little bit was good, a little more must be better. Progressively, we build up an unhealthy disrespect for those things we know are best for us.*

little more must be better. Progressively, we build up an unhealthy disrespect for the things we know are best for us. Before we know it, we are heading over the cliff and falling helplessly to an unknown fate.

Such was the case for Samson. Samson was born for one purpose – to deliver the Israelites from the oppression of the Midianites. Although he was gifted, or maybe because he was gifted, it appeared that he lacked a respect for the call upon his life. In the sixteenth chapter of the book of the Judges, the Scriptures recount Samson's game of chess with a person who had more at stake than a fun time. Playing for her life and the life of her family, Delilah continually pressed Samson for the source of his strength. Instead of taking the stance of the third driver mentioned earlier by getting as far away as possible from the threat of danger, Samson remained in the presence of the temptation. Day after day, Delilah continued to question him until eventually Samson caved in and revealed it all. Enslaved upon capture, he ended up losing his sight, his dignity, and his life. Worse yet, he was unable to fulfill the very purpose for which he was born and his nation remained in bondage.

As a former Safety Specialist, I have often shared with co-workers that accidents are normally the result of a chain of circumstances and causes. Typically, there are several warning signs of areas that suggest trouble ahead. When we remain in environments where there are real or perceived dangers, or something that threatens our intended outcome, we are deciding that we are bigger than the consequences.

Instead of succumbing to the appeal of the moment and progressively being led as sheep to the slaughter, when we receive evidence of things that seem awry, we need to make the necessary adjustments as quickly as possible to get back on the right track.

Purpose

Chapter 20

‒‒‒‒‒‒

*P**urpose* – There are miracles in having a life of purpose. Developing a burning desire to fulfill that which God has called you to do is the starting point of achievement. Too many of us have been duped into believing that unless we have a *major* purpose in life, our time on earth does not matter. This mindset could not be further from the truth. For every nation of Israel who desires deliverance from the hands of their Egyptian masters, God seeks a Moses. For every Civil Rights movement confronting racial inequality, God seeks a Martin Luther King, Jr. And for every Jackie, God seeks someone who will listen to His voice, and respond obediently.

I fondly recall hearing a story from a young lady who told me that God's Spirit prompted her to act, and she did. The outcome – her suicidal neighbor Jackie, survived the night and is still here today. Let me recount the story:

She told me that she had a long day and had decided to come home and go straight to bed. Well, it did not work out as she planned. She worked on her computer and had the window of her 2nd floor dorm room open. For about 30 minutes she heard a girl crying out from the adjacent window. Instead of the situation sounding like it was getting better; it seemed to escalate until she finally heard a door slam and the lights abruptly went off. For some time, she felt God's

Spirit prompting her to say something, but she tried to ignore Him.

> *Each one of us has been placed on this earth to accomplish a specific purpose and I believe God is counting on us to come through.*

Finally, unable to ignore the pressing inside of her, she lifted the blinds and said "Hello." There was no response. She called out again, "Hello." A whimpering voice came to the window. "I heard you crying and I just wanted to know if you were okay." Jackie began crying even louder. She told the concerned neighbor that she had been contemplating the best way to commit suicide. She had gotten drunk and taken some aspirin so she would not feel the pain. She had tied a computer power cord in her shower, ready to hang herself. Just before hearing the neighbor's voice calling out to her, she had shut the door, turned off the lights, and had a knife, priming to cut her wrist.

To God, I believe obedience from someone who made herself available to Jackie was just as significant as obedience from Moses and John the Baptizer. Everyone will not make the *Forbes 100 Most Influential People* list, or the *Time Magazine's Person of the Year*. For many of us, our encounter with the Jackie's of the world will never be captured on film or in print.

Each one of us has been placed on this earth to accomplish a specific purpose and I believe God is counting on us to come through. Often, God will invest a great deal of time grooming and preparing us for specific moments in which He will reveal to us what we are to do. Paraphrasing Rick Warren's opening statement in his book, *The Purpose Driven Life*, "It is not about us." It is about being available to God to fulfill the call that He has placed upon us and making sure that when He calls, we are willing and obedient to answer and fulfill His purpose.

Positive

Chapter 21

Positive – I once heard of an exchange between a father and a son regarding the son's grades. "Dad, I think I failed my last exam," the son hesitantly explained. The dad replied, "Son, that is no way to think. You have to be positive about how you did." The son responded, "Dad, I am positive I failed my last exam." There are some things you may have to think about. There are other things you just know.

I am reminded of a quote by Vince Lombardi when asked about losing games. Vince's thoughts were that he never lost a game, he simply ran out of time. Regardless of how positive Vince felt about the outcome of the game, the final scoreboard showed a victory for the other team. How does one balance a positive outlook with reality? At what point does the curtain fall and the show comes to an end with no encore?

For years, I have heard speakers proclaim the importance of having a positive mental attitude. I adopted the concept – hook, line, and sinker. I cannot explain the difference it has made in my life to look for the good in

Remaining positive is a requirement if we are to overcome all of the situations and obstacles we will face in this journey called "Life."

situations. This has proven beneficial in many situations in my life. However, the same outlook that has blessed me often, I also think of as one of my biggest weaknesses. I have said it in various settings; I may be optimistic to a fault. Because of my belief in people and in myself, there have been many challenges when the appropriate response would have been to pull the plug and cut my losses. But since I believe the outcome is always going to get better given enough time, I may fail to act in a timely manner and end up losing out on something that could yield a more desirable return.

Of all of the *P Attitudes* covered in this book, the one that possesses the greatest ability to stimulate the others is *Positive*. Remaining positive is a requirement if we are to overcome situations and obstacles we face in this journey called "Life." In the words of all the brothers and sisters from my home church who would give their "testimony," life is full of "trials and tribulations." A positive outlook is the catalyst for activating all of the other attitudes. In chemistry and biology, **catalysis** is a way of accelerating the rate of a chemical reaction by means of contacting the reactants with a substance called a **catalyst**, which itself is not consumed by the overall reaction. [1]

Other than Christ Jesus, I cannot think of another person in the New Testament who endured as much hardship and opposition than the Apostle Paul. Paul discloses his laundry list of calamities. He speaks of "…stripes above measure, in prisons more frequently, in deaths often. From the Jews five times I received forty stripes minus one. Three times I was beaten with rods; once I was stoned; three times I was shipwrecked; a night and a day I have been in the deep; in journeys often, in perils of water, in perils of robbers, in perils of my own countrymen, in perils of the Gentiles, in perils in the

---

[1] http://en.wikipedia.org/wiki/Catalyst

city, in perils in the wilderness, in perils in the sea, in perils among false brethren; in weariness and toil, in sleeplessness often, in hunger and thirst, in fastings often, in cold and nakedness" (2 Corinthians 11:23-27 NKJV). Regardless of the severity of his sufferings, Paul remained positive about the expected outcome. In a letter to his protégé Timothy, Paul encourages Timothy to remain positive. Paul states, "…for I know in whom I have believed and am persuaded that He is able to keep what I have committed to Him until that Day" (2 Timothy 1:12b NKJV).

Under normal circumstances, one could easily understand if Paul lost hope during these most challenging times. However, Paul understood truth. Because he recognized that the difficult times in his life were only temporary inconveniences, it was easy for him to make the decision to endure the light affliction. There was a greater, more eternal weight of glory that he would receive. Paul did not have exclusive rights to this promise. It is available to all those who love and anticipate the Lord's coming. Christ is coming back. We do not have to think about it – we can know it. A positive attitude is like the additive to the fuel that helps the "gears" of the other attitudes continue to turn.

Powerful

Chapter 22

—◦◦◦—

Powerful – Paraphrasing a quote from Prime Minister Margaret Thatcher, "Being powerful is like being a lady. If you have to tell someone that you are, you probably are not." I once remember hearing a story of Muhammad Ali being challenged by a small child – the child threatened to whip Ali. Obviously, because Ali knew who was the more powerful of the two, he did not concern himself with the child's threat.

Being in a position of power has a great deal of responsibility associated with it. A good way to determine a person's character is to watch how they handle power. It is easy to get someone to go along with you when they are afraid of you. However, a truly powerful person is the one who understands that fear alone cannot secure a following, for if fear is the only motivation; their position is secure only until someone with more power comes along.

During my college days, I played intramural football. I was known more for my speed than my size. At five feet, nine inches, and weighing in at a whopping 165 pounds, it was easy to see that I did not intimidate many people because of my *imposing* figure. During one contest, there was a player on the opposite team who was significantly larger than me, as well as most of my teammates. And he did not mind pushing the limits of the flag football game by roughing up some of our guys. Our team was holding our own in the score, but losing heart because of this guy's intimidating style of play. Eventually, I had enough. I am not

> We are created in the image and likeness of God. We are powerful because He is powerful.

sure what rose up inside of me but before I knew it, I had run full speed, with the force of every fiber of my being, into this guy, knocking him to the ground. He was shocked. His teammates were stunned. My teammates were elated. I extended my hand and helped him up. After making sure he was okay, we exchanged a sportsman-like glance of respect at each other and the game continued. From that point on, there was no more rough play from that guy or any of his teammates.

We are daily focused with intimidating scenarios. The economic condition is threatening. Job security may be suspect. Health issues, financial woes, relationship challenges, all can give us the impression that we are being bullied around by things over which we have little or no control. But that is not the case. Eleanor Roosevelt said, "No one can make you feel inferior without your consent." I believe the statement can be expanded to say, "No thing can make you feel inferior without your consent." Some people are afraid of electronics. Some are intimidated by computers. Some people feel powerless because of their fear of flying, but we are created in the image and likeness of God. We are powerful because He is powerful. We were created to rule and to have dominion over the earth and all of its inhabitants.

At the time of his arrest, Christ was confronted by the Jewish leaders and the Roman soldiers. Unwilling to see Christ taken into captivity without a fight, Peter drew his sword and cut off the ear of one of the soldiers. Christ rebuked him and told him to sheath his sword, and reminded him that people who have to resort to displays of power and might to accomplish their goals will be consumed by the very power they use. "Or do you think that I cannot now pray to My Father, and He will provide me with more than twelve legions of angels?" (Matthew 26:53 NKJV) Christ realized that the time to display His power would soon come. If Christ were to release His power out of the appropriate season, it would circumvent the plan for His life. He also knew that NO ONE could take His Power.

When you are confident that you already possess the power to overcome any situation, you do not have to feel inferior to anyone or intimidated by anything. Christ, at His resurrection, promised us power to overcome. The promise of power comes in the presence of the Holy Spirit. Because we already possess that power, we do not have to worry about someone having to give us power. We are powerful through the All-Powerful One.

Priceless

Chapter 23

—✷✷✷—

*P*riceless – "Life is not fair." If I had a nickel for every time I heard someone spout out this phrase, I would be doing very well financially. To make matters worse, the statement is true. There really is nothing "fair" about life. The more I think about it, the more I am convinced that is the way it should be.

I have a confession to make; my life has not been fair. I have to admit that I have been blessed beyond anything I could have ever imagined. I have two loving parents, who have been married for over 50 years. I have a loving and supportive wife and three adorable children. My siblings and I enjoy each other's company and are willing to help out whenever there is a need. The family support structure my parents provided for us is unlike any I have ever seen. My health has been great. I have been "favored" throughout life. For me these surroundings have created a truly priceless environment.

Before I paint an unrealistic picture, there is something else that should be factored into this story. Calvin Dean was my older brother. Priscilla Anne was my older sister. These are two of my siblings who died at an early age. Calvin died before I was born. My first memory of life was Anne's funeral. I never knew my dad's parents. My best friend in high school committed suicide during college. I have lost friends, relatives, and mentors. My family has had our share of tragedy and unfortunate situations. It was out of those situations, however, that we grew closer and

> *Adversity, when introduced into the right atmosphere, is the polishing cloth that creates character.*

developed an understanding that it was our relationships that was our treasure. I came to realize that "family matters."

I think that many people have used the logic of them being a product of their environment. I have to believe that while there may be some truth to those sentiments, I also understand that we have been afforded an opportunity that is unavailable to any of the rest of God's creation. We can choose our response to our situations. During my parent's retirement celebration, there were people who shared stories about how poor my family was during my childhood. However, I would not trade a day of my life with anyone. Today, I understand that every uncertain moment, every shared meal, every pair of second-hand clothes, every trip to Jonesville, every reduced or free lunch; for me, the entire experience was priceless.

Although I believe fully in the "Creation" version of man's existence as opposed to a "big bang" theory or evolution, I do agree that there is some logic to the "survival of the fittest" concept. There are some universal laws that apply and there are consequences for complying to and for violating these laws. One of the laws that I believe creates an attitude of appreciation is an understanding that adversity, when introduced into the right atmosphere, is the polishing cloth that creates character. Borrowing an overly used cliché, "Hard times can make you bitter, or hard times can make you better." The choice is yours. "John," some might ask, "What about those people who are victims through no fault of their own?" My response is this, "In one way or another, we all have been put in situations or we will be put in situations where we could become a victim. That is the way it is."

Before I am accused of being cold and callous, let me explain. There are some situations where my heart is moved with compassion for people who are involved in calamities through which they have no control. There are other people who create unfortunate situations through their actions. We are all one wrong decision away from having our lives turned "proverbially" upside down. I have said repeatedly, "The only difference between my life and the lives of every one else on this earth is the decisions – those that have been made by me, those that have been made about me, and those that have been made for me." That is the beauty of it – God has given us a chance to choose. That is why I have come to realize that life is priceless. MasterCard had the right idea when they said there are some things that money can buy, but other things are priceless.

Pride

Chapter 24

— ◈ —

Pride – STOP. Road Out Ahead. Sharp Turn. Falling Rocks. There are signs of impending danger in almost every city. Our government has laws that mandate the kind of signs we are to install to protect the public from possible danger. We have agencies that enforce compliance of what is posted. Sadly, many people lose their lives every year because they fail to heed the warning signs. What we do not have is an agency that enforces our obedience to the signs that have been erected for our protection. Many people feel they do not have the heed to the signs.

The book of Proverbs in the Bible says that the Lord hates a proud look. Hate, in this context expressed as an emotion from God, is not to be taken lightly. However, this is the same God who called out from heaven to those gathered around the Jordan River to witness Christ's baptism, "You are My beloved Son; in You I am well pleased. (Luke 3:22 NKJV). It could easily be argued that God was telling all of those who listened that He was proud of His Son, Jesus. So, what is it about the prideful heart that angers God to the point that He hates the very look of it?

There is something that takes place in the heart of a person filled with pride that suggests self-sufficiency. Whenever a person is confronted with logic, reason and/or truth, but still refuses to hear, I can only conclude that the person has decided that they have all the answers; that there are no grounds for entertaining any other opinion. I can

> *It's of little value to me to be right, or to feel that I am right if it results in the loss of my life.*

assure you that whenever you come across a person like this, you are looking at someone who is in trouble but does not know it. Any time you find a person who has all the answers, regardless of what the question is, this is a dangerous person – to himself and those who are unfortunate enough to be around him.

During high school, I took a Driver's Education course. We were studying the "Yield" sign. One of the statements my teacher made that left a lasting impression on me was to cautiously approach the "Yield" sign. He said that a driver may have the right-of-way, but could still end up in a crash. In this situation, the driver could be "dead right." I got the message. It is of little value to me to be right, or to feel that I am right if it results in the loss of my life.

As a teenager, I had a basketball that was given to me by my parents. We lived across from the community park and so it was often that the neighborhood children would come to borrow our ball to play on the court. Because we often loaned out the ball, I wrote my name on it. On one occasion, the guys who borrowed the ball left it on the court and one of the neighborhood children "found" it. When I went to the court to play basketball, I told the guy that the ball belonged to me; it had my name on it. The other guy said it was his. We disagreed over the rightful owner. Since our negotiations were producing little result, the other guy decided he would leave. Thinking I had won, you can imagine my surprise when he reappeared with a rifle. Once again, he suggested the ball rightfully belonged to him. All of a sudden, I realized that I had a problem with my reading because the name on the ball began to look amazingly similar to how he spelled his name. He got the ball because I realized that it was of little value to be "dead right."

The Pharisees and Sadducees of Christ's day refused to hear the truth. They were more concerned about holding on to their positions of status than they were about hearing a message that could save their lives. Repeatedly, Christ gave them the opportunity to hear a different message than that which they were familiar – the truth. Christ said on many occasions, "Verily, I tell you the truth." Nicodemus was willing to lay aside his pride for the sake of hearing what the Lord had to say. Although the message was difficult for him to process, he was open to hearing it. The Pharisees who failed to accept Christ's teaching were, in their own minds, right. Unfortunately, they were "dead right."

Promise

Chapter 25

—◦◦◦—

*P*romise – If you had the choice, would you rather receive a miracle or a promise? I imagine your response would depend on knowing what the miracle was, as well as knowing who made the promise. Maybe this will help clear it up. A miracle would be winning the lottery. If you are the lucky recipient, your life could be drastically changed. Unfortunately, as I have heard, you stand a better chance of being hit by lightning than winning the lottery. A promise, on the other hand, is consistently investing in a mutual fund over many years and realizing a guaranteed six or seven percent return for twenty-five or thirty years.

All things being equal, I would rather have a fulfilled promise than a miracle. One reality I have come to understand is that people who need miracles are normally in dire straits. There is usually no where else to turn and if something does not come through for them, their situation remains hopeless. When a person makes and keeps a promise, it is like a breath of fresh air.

So why do we put so little confidence and faith in the promises that are made to us? Is it because we have had so many broken promises made that we have lost confidence in people? In a society where so many people consistently over promise and under deliver, it is easy to see why we are so suspicious when anyone makes us a promise. We have

> *The Creator of heaven and earth has a reputation. He delivers on His promises.*

heard it before, "If it sounds too good to be true, it probably is not." There are advertising campaigns aimed at getting our money. "Lose 30 pounds in three days or your money back, guaranteed." There are political campaigns determined to garner our votes. "Vote for me and I promise to end unemployment, homelessness, and provide free insurance to all who need it." Through deceptive tactics and ill-willed intents, a culture has been created where there is little trust and belief in others.

How do we determine which promises to believe in? What is it that we look for? What if there was someone who has consistently kept His word? What if the track record revealed that this person has never broken a promise? Could we place our trust in Him? Would we place our confidence in Him? This person exists indeed. Here are some of the testimonies spoken about His reputation:

"God is not a man, that He should lie, nor a son of man, that He should repent. Has He said, and will He not do? Or has He spoken, and will He not make it good?" (Numbers 23:19 NKJV)

"Blessed be the Lord, who has given rest to His people, Israel, according to all He promised. There has not failed one word of all His good promise, which He promised through His servant Moses" (1 Kings 8:56 NKJV).

"The Lord is not slack concerning His promise, as some count slackness, but is longsuffering toward us, not willing that any should perish but that all should come to repentance" (2 Peter 3:9 NKJV)

There are hundreds and hundreds of promises made by God for His children. He has ordained us as heirs to those promises by faith. If we are not aware of the promises, or if we fail to believe the promises, then they are of no value to us. A promise is only as good as the one who has made the promise. The Creator of heaven and earth has a reputation. He delivers on His promises!

Perform

Chapter 26

—❦—

Perform – When it is all said and done, you can either perform the required functions or you can not. If the minimum required typing speed for a position is 35 correct words per minute (CWPM), there is a simple typing test to measure your performance against a pre-established requirement. If your typing score is 34 CWPM or less, your performance did not meet the required standard. If your score is 35 CWPM or more, your performance allowed you to pass that portion of the screening process and you were permitted to proceed further along in the process.

There have been many times in my life when I became consumed with wanting to know all of the steps involved in a project before I knew whether or not I could do the first step. Surely, no one would ever argue the value of planning ahead and counting the costs. It is humorous when someone during a job application and interview process, asks about the 30-year retirement program. I would think that the focus would be to determine what I need to do to secure the position and then learn how to perform all of the essential functions of the

> *His response to me was, "Finish writing the book!"*

job. Even if I were selected for the position, if at any time during my career, I fail to continue to perform at the level established, I could be given an opportunity to pursue other employment options. If I ever reach a point where my performance exceeds the requirements for my current position, then I may still be afforded an opportunity to pursue other career options. In one case, my pursuit may lead me up the ladder. The option may lead me out the door.

One morning, while in prayer regarding writing this book, one of my questions to my Father was, "What am I going to do about getting this book published?" His response to me was, "Finish writing the book." Of course my immediate thought was that I really needed to know the rest of the steps so I can have some idea of what else was required – who should I contact to publish? Should I self publish? How much money is it going to cost? Who should I contact to see where I can find the money in case it costs more than I have at the time? As quickly as I had those thoughts, another thought came to mind. None of this matters if I do not finish writing the book.

It is so easy to get off focus from the things we should really be concentrating on. There are so many things that need to be done that each of us can do. A question that often continues to dominate our minds is, "What should I do – now?" It is imperative that we pause long enough to get an answer. We have to determine just what it is that I am supposed to do that is necessary to achieve the ultimate outcome. Once we determine what that main thing is, then we are to do all we can to perform in a manner that ensures we reach the goal.

During the time of the early church, the message of Jesus spread and the number of disciples multiplied. As a result, there were some complaints filed by one of the new groups because they felt their widows were being neglected. When it was brought to the disciples' attention, they realized that although the complaint was legitimate, it was not in the best interest of the mission for *them* to perform those duties. They instructed the brothers who were concerned about the issue to find other capable men who possessed the needed character and skill to perform those tasks. The disciples would continue doing the thing that all agreed was critical to the mission. As a result of the disciples' decision to perform in the area where they were most needed, and allow others an opportunity to operate in other areas, the widows' needs were met and the word of God was spread across the nation.

Regardless of whether or not you see your role as critical to the mission, when you commit to perform in the area where you have specific gifts and abilities, you open up opportunities for others to perform in their gifted area. The end result – mission accomplished!

Precious

Chapter 27

—◁◁◁—

Precious – This day will most likely be etched in my memory forever. I had been expecting the call for several days now, maybe even a week. However, when it came I still could barely believe it. It was about 7:30 in the morning when the phone rang. "John, you need to meet us at the hospital. She is in labor; I think she is about to have the baby." I had worked the night before so my wife stayed with her sister because we knew that she could deliver our daughter at any moment. I like to think that I reacted calmly and rationally. I changed the message on my answering machine so that anyone who called would know that I was about to be a daddy!

After about six hours of labor, which went by in a blur for me, all of a sudden, every-thing in the room went into slow

> *If the children were not taught their history, there would be nothing to keep them grounded when they were exposed to so many confusing and contradictory messages.*

motion. Immediately after delivery, with some cleaning of the lungs and other fluids, the nurse turned around and handed my daughter, whom I call "Precious," to me. I can honestly say from that moment, nothing in my life has been the same. Being in the delivery room for the birth of my children has created indelible sets of precious memories.

There have been many other moments that when I slow down enough to reflect on them, have caused me to close my eyes and take a deep sigh. A smile flashes across my face and, as my dad would say, "I get a little warm and mushy feeling in the center of my chest."

As a child, it was expected that I attended church. We had a small congregation, but there were so many exceptional people there. Each year during the month of March, we hosted a commemorative program called "Old Fashioned Day." It was always a highly emotional service. We would dress as closely as we could to the way our patriarchs and matriarchs dressed. We sung the same songs they used to sing. We turned off the air conditioner and opened the windows so we could feel the breeze and smell the scent of spring. The purpose of that service was to make sure the legacy of our forefathers was never forgotten by each successive generation. Someone understood that if the children were not taught their history, there would be nothing to keep them grounded when they were exposed to the many confusing and contradictory messages. What wonderful, precious memories.

That is the same message Moses kept rehearsing with the Israelites in the book of Deuteronomy. Teach your children the mighty works of God so they would not forget Him. Remind them constantly of His miraculous feats so they would know to depend on Him and not their own might or abilities. Moses reminded them of how hard things used to be. For over four hundred years, you were enslaved by the Egyptians before God delivered you – His precious children. When you were surrounded by the Red Sea in front of you and Pharaoh's army behind, God supernaturally intervened. When you had no food, God provided. Your garments and sandals were kept for forty years. When you were cold, He provided heat. When you were hot, He provided shelter. This is the God you are to rely on in the future. Remember Him and teach your children to remember Him also.

So many times, in the rush to meet this deadline and make that appointment, we are too busy to slow down and reflect. I am not suggesting that we live in the past. We must learn from it. We have heard it before – those who do not learn from the past are destined to repeat it. In other words, if we don't learn from the past, we *are* going to relive it. Do I want to go back to the "good ol' days?" I am not sure; but there is one thing I am sure about – I love to go back and think about them. As the traditional gospel says, "Precious memories, how they linger; how they ever flood my soul. In the stillness of the midnight, precious, sacred scenes unfold."

Praise

Chapter 28

Praise – Although someone can give praise to you – no one can give praise for you. I find it so interesting that throughout the scriptures, offering of praise has always been a choice of the individual. The Psalms are full of the phrase, "I will ... praise." In each case, the writer displays a resolve, a decision, a choice to praise. Choosing an attitude of praise is a right that each individual has.

Praise is an act of worship or acknowledgement by which the virtues or deeds of another are recognized or extolled. To praise is to appraise or esteem; to express a favorable judgment of. Sincere praise has the ability to change a person's perception of themselves.

Each of my children has unique and adorable traits. My oldest daughter is a self-professed recovering people pleaser. She operates with a spirit of excellence with an uncanny attention to detail. My youngest daughter has a heart of compassion. She is gifted with the ability to empathize with other's feelings, even when those feelings are not verbally expressed. My son is as charismatic as a successful politician. He does not know what it means to be at odds with people. He has the ability to endear himself to almost anyone who is sincerely looking for a friend.

One thing they all have in common, however, is a desire to be praised. In fact, I will go as far as to say that they have a need to be praised; and they are deserving of it. It is my choice to make sure each of them knows that I value them. I understand the power of a supportive smile. I realize how it makes me feel when the people I admire and respect most give me feedback on how I am doing. It does not harm me in any way to say something kind and uplifting to my children; to offer a word of praise to them in an activity of their choice. It could very well mean the world to them to know that their dad is their biggest fan.

During the winter holidays, my family has a tradition of getting together for dinner. During this time, we often take a moment

> *Each individual has something that is worthy of praise. Our job is to find out what it is and make sure we share it with the person.*

before dinner to allow each person an opportunity to express his or her feelings if they so desire. One thing my brothers, sisters, nieces, and nephews could always depend on was hearing my dad and mom tell us how proud they were of us. Those words lasted so much longer than the food we ate or the gifts we exchanged. The thing that solidified the process for me was hearing my nieces and nephews sharing how much they appreciated the model my parents and siblings have been to them. It is during those times of praise when one comes to appreciate the value of being a person of worth.

Unfortunately, I realize that not everyone understands how damaging words are when they are spoken with evil and selfish motives. Instead of praising, some criticize and literally rip hope, courage, and a sense of accomplishment away from an individual. After King David had successfully returned the Ark of God from Obed Edom's house to the City of David, David rejoiced mightily. He took off his royal robe and danced in the streets with all the house of Israel.

His wife Michal, was embarrassed by David's actions; she despised him in her heart. Instead of praising him for successfully bringing the Ark home, she spoke spitefully to him. "How glorious was the king of Israel today, uncovering himself today in the eyes of the maids of his servants as one of the base fellows shamelessly uncovers himself!" (2 Samuel 6:20b NKJV) As a result of her refusal to praise, she ended up childless for the rest of her life.

I once heard a wise and very successful salesman share some wisdom on why he was able to close so many sale transactions. He said there is something beautiful in every person; it was his job to find it and to point it out to the customer. Once the customer understood that he was as interested in them as an individual as he was in making the sale, they were more willing to take his opinion on the product that he suggested would best meet their needs.

Each individual has something that is worthy of praise. Our job is to find out what it is and make sure we share it with them. Our goal may not be to make a sale. Maybe we can make a difference. Maybe we can make a friend.

Perceive

Chapter 29

—⟨o⟩o⟨o⟩—

Perceive – There are some people who seem to "get it" quicker than others. These people are able to survey a situation and quickly surmise what is going on. I love being around those people. I have found that this personality style is able to gather the facts, process the information presented, and make a decision, without needing to call a committee together to discuss every minute detail. Some call it insight, intuition, or a sixth-sense. I call it a joy!

Then there are other people who seem as if they could not "get it" if "it" was a big hole that they literally fell into. It does not matter how many times the vision is shared, or the different ways you communicate the message. It is like talking to an Idaho potato. I have found this to be a highly frustrating event, not only for me, but also for the person with whom I have intended to make a connection.

In *The 21 Irrefutable Laws of Leadership*, John C. Maxwell calls it a leadership law – the Law of Intuition. He asserts that this is a difficult law to place under your belt because this skill requires a collection of facts and faith. He states that a leader's strength in this area will follow most closely to the leader's natural area of giftedness, or their spiritual gift. What excited me most as I familiarized myself with his concept, was that he convinced me that I can learn to be insightful. I could become more accurate in my ability to perceive people and situations.

As a former wedding photographer, it was often intriguing to meet with the ecstatic couple prior to that joyful day. It was so amusing to see them discuss the activities for the day when their lives would be "joined together in holy matrimony." In many cases, after just a brief exchange with the couple, it was easy to discern who was calling the shots. In most cases I could tell whether or not the wedding was a case of joining two individuals who were truly in love with each other and were looking for a long-term union or two people who were getting ready to spend a lot of money on an event that was more an exercise in futility. Although there was no fool-proof method for making the determination, there were several factors that could be used to help establish a sound baseline. I considered the current circumstances. There is a lot of pressure in planning a marriage. I looked at the people involved and how they related to each other; I sensed their tones and temperaments; I also factored in my previous experiences and I was right more often than not.

On several occasions, the Jewish leaders approached Christ to attempt to trick Him into saying something that they could use as evidence to turn the people against Him. They asked His opinion on governmental affairs. They wanted to know what He thought about spiritual matters. He was asked to comment on relational issues. They tried every possible tactic they could think of that could be used to create controversy and cause some dissension in the crowd. They were never successful because in each instance, Christ was able to perceive what was in their hearts and keep them from achieving their desired end.

One of the advantages for the person who possesses this trait is the ability to relate to the situation. They are available to assist others, who have the right motives, to move through the process by bringing attention to areas that might have otherwise been missed. In spite of our best intentions, we are not going to be one hundred percent accurate in how we perceive things all of the time. However, when we are, it is as soothing as a soft rain shower on a blistering, summer day; it refreshes everything in its vicinity.

Possibilities

Chapter 30

—◁〇〇〇▷—

Possibilities – I have often conducted a training program called, "Conflict Resolution." In many cases I had to employ some of the principles from those sessions in my personal life. One of the lessons I learned was to be careful when giving your version of the interaction and avoid using phrases that contain words such as "always" and "never." Both of these words leave no room for an out. In all of the relationships and disagreements that I know of, I cannot think of a single time when one person "always" did one thing and the other person "never" did something else.

From whence do possibilities come? There are several ingredients. Possibilities are like the cakes baked by a loving mother's hands. There are many ingredients that make up possibilities which all revolve around one theme – the fruit of the Spirit; love, joy, peace, longsuffering, kindness, goodness, faithfulness, gentleness, and self-control. Each baker has some other items they add to the recipe that gives the delicacy its own special touch. A couple of things I like to add to possibilities are hope, trust, belief, imagination, dreams, forgiveness, resilience, wisdom, and commitment.

Possibilities exist in the couple on their wedding day. Two people who have waited for God to unite them live for possibilities. Parents, holding their newborn child anticipate the possibilities. The graduate, after enduring four, six, or eight years of college, predicts the possibilities. The employee, on the first day of the new job, or maybe the last day before retirement, foresees possibilities.

> *Until we breathe our last breath, there is always a chance for things to turn around; we are never out of options.*

Maybe it's the new business owner preparing for the grand opening, or the little child joining a grandparent for their first fishing trip. We find people longing for possibilities in every walk of life.

Are there some situations when it is okay to use terms like "always" and "never?" I think so. There was a father who had a demon-possessed son. The father desperately wanted his son delivered. Christ's disciples were unsuccessful in bringing deliverance to the child. When the child was brought to Jesus, the father pleaded for Christ to do something. He begged for Christ to show compassion to the child. Jesus said to him, "If you can believe, *all* things are possible to him who believes." (Mark 9:23 NKJV)

We are being conformed into the image of Jesus. I believe we have been created to reach for something bigger, something better, something supernatural. We have been given authority to use the name of Jesus to take dominion over situations, turning them around and bringing them in alignment with the will of God. I understand, however, that this requires that we walk in the fruit of the Spirit. We have to know what it is that God requires and then we have to do what we know.

Until we breathe our last breath, there is always a chance for things to turn around; we are never out of options. **Because of who we are in Christ, the possibilities related to our lives are endless.**